ARTIFICIAL INTELLIGENCE

Prosperity or Robo-Apocalypse?

David Parsons

Naples, Florida

November 16, 2017

ISBN-13: 978-1975712792

ISBN-10: 197571279X

CONTENTS

Preface

In February of 2017, I agreed to give a talk on the future of artificial intelligence (AI) as part of the Grey Oaks[1] lifelong learning program. This subject has been popular in the press with much speculation about the future impact of AI. Once I took on the project, it seemed like news coverage about artificial intelligence was everywhere. As I began to review the many stories about self-driving cars or breakthroughs in medical diagnosis or application of AI to a myriad of human tasks, I began to realize that I did not really understand what was behind the curtain. Aside from knowing references to *deep learning* or *semantic algorithms*, the coverage gave me no sense of whether this was really something new, or just regular old computer programming running on faster and faster machines.

In that light, I decided that what I wanted for me, and for my esteemed lifelong learners, was to understand what really makes AI work. I felt capable of exploring this area having learned many programming languages, including assembly languages dating from the early 1960s. It is helpful that I have kept in touch over the decades with the work of several prominent contributors to this field.

---

[1] Grey Oaks Country Club, Naples, Florida.

Turns out, there is lot behind the curtain. It has been a challenge to sort this out and find the right way to present it to a very capable, diverse and curious group of my peers. This book is my safety net. In this format, I hope I can pull the curtain all the way back, recognizing that a one-hour presentation will leave much unexplored.

1. INTRODUCTION

Artificial
intelligence
(AI)

If you can read the words above there is a good chance you are not a robot, unless your software was written within the last five years. Why can humans read this so easily, but the use of contorted letters throws computers off? Our ability to recognize objects, including letters, that are distortions of what we have seen before gives a clue as to the difference between the way our mind works and the way computers work. This difference is not a small thing. It underlies the difficulty that computers have had doing many tasks that humans find easy.

What is Intelligence?

The Oxford English Dictionary defines intelligence as follows:

> *Intelligence: The ability to acquire and apply knowledge and skills*

This simple definition puts learning and action at the center of intelligence. The ability to acquire knowledge and skills implies an inherent drive for exploration and understanding.

The ability to apply knowledge and skills implies the ability to predict outcomes. There is also learning *from* action – observing the results of action to improve one's knowledge and skills. You might ask: where is creativity, curiosity, and logical thinking? I suggest that these have emerged in service of the ability to acquire knowledge and skills.

It follows that intelligence of the artificial kind, that housed in computers, should be able to learn, predict, act and observe the results of its actions to improve its knowledge and skills. So how is AI coming along?

Robocalypse? (Robot-Apocalypse)

Over the last eight decades, artificial intelligence (AI) has evolved from a glimmer in the eye of science fiction writers to the beginnings of widespread application in every corner of our lives. With ever expanding computing power, some thinkers fear that artificial intelligence will ultimately surpass human intelligence with dire consequences. Should we be concerned?

You may have noticed that there is a lot of concern in the press about the impact of artificial intelligence. Will it take our jobs? Will computers be able to think like people? Will computers exterminate us for our own good? Famed physicist Steven Hawking has talked of the **end of the human race**! In 2014, he offered the following:

The development of full artificial intelligence could spell the end of the human race.... It would take off on its own, and re-design itself at an ever-increasing rate. Humans, who are limited by slow biological evolution, couldn't compete, and would be superseded.

Elon Musk, founder of SpaceX and the car company, Tesla, has called artificial intelligence our biggest existential threat.

I think we should be very careful about artificial intelligence. If I had to guess at what our biggest existential threat is, it's probably that.

Mark Zuckerberg of Facebook takes a far more optimistic view of the future of AI. He responded to Musk's dark vision with the following comments:

I think people who are naysayers and try to drum up these doomsday scenarios — I don't understand it. It's really negative, and in some ways, I think it's pretty irresponsible.

Paul Allen, Microsoft co-founder, has been a big player in the development of AI. He founded the Allen Institute for Artificial Intelligence, funding it at a level of $500 million. He has also provided substantial funding for AI research at Cal Tech. He reassuringly offers that AI will not exterminate us.

The technology will not exterminate humans but empower them, making humans more inventive and helping solve huge global problems such as climate change.

The goal of this small book is to help you understand what artificial intelligence is so that you can consider for yourself the impact it might have on the future of the people you care about. With book in hand, I am hoping you will be able to make your own sense of the sometimes contradictory stories in the press about AI.

To understand AI, first we have to understand a bit about the strengths and weaknesses of computers, the place where AI lives. Second, we have to understand a bit about how the human brain works, particularly the cerebral cortex where most of what passes for human intelligence lives. We will see that the basic architecture of the brain and the computer are radically different.

The big question in artificial intelligence is: should we be trying to get computers to think the way humans do. There have been two answers to that question, both of them YES. The first is what I am calling RULE-BASED AI, which sees the brain as a logical thinking machine. Its foundation is built on looking for the rules by which humans go about solving problems. The second is NEURON-BASED AI, an effort to capture how we think at the level of the billions of neurons that make up our brain. This approach sees intelligence as emerging from the structure of the neo-cortex.

We are going to try to understand both of these forms of AI, and their potential for changing the way we work and live.

Why should we be paying attention to artificial intelligence?

I am seventy-six years old. I'm hoping that by the time my kids try to hide my car keys, self-driving cars will be a reality. But my main interest in AI is about my kids and their kids. Over the next forty years, AI will flourish. My kids, Andrew and Jennifer, will have to adapt in their personal and work lives to ever-increasing AI capabilities. They seem to be in good shape to handle this evolution. Their kids, Nora, Emmy, Desi, and Violet will move into a world potentially shaped by AI. Will this be a world further divided into the haves and have nots? Will humans begin to suffer a massive inferiority complex? What does this future hold?

The Evolution of Artificial Intelligence

Let me introduce you to a brief history of AI from when it was a glimmer in the eye of science fiction writers like Isaac Asimov, through decades of gradual development at universities, to now when thousands of young people are being trained to engineer artificial intelligence solutions in every sector of our lives.

Science Fiction

In 1942, before the invention of the programmable computer, Isaac Asimov wrote of robots and their intelligence. He was concerned, as many folks are today, about how robots would behave as they approach and perhaps exceed human intelligence. In his short story, *Runaround*, he wrote of a future time when robot behavior would be controlled by the three laws of robotics. In Asimov's future world, these laws were documented in the Handbook of Robotics published in 2058. The laws were enforced by programming them into the positronic brains of all robots.

- A robot may not injure a human being
- A robot must obey the orders given it by human beings
- A robot must protect its own existence

Movies have portrayed robots in more and more human form, from Robbie in *Forbidden Planet*, to C3PIO in *Star Wars*, to Sonny in the movie *I, Robot*, based on the Asimov novel by the same name. But the current reality of AI takes more the form of Amazon's Echo (Alexa) or Google's self-driving car.

People are using the terms *Robot* and *artificial intelligence* interchangeably, even though robots in manufacturing do not necessarily use AI, and AI often does not take human form, or for that matter any physical form outside of a computer. I will generally use the term artificial intelligence to refer to any contrivance that exhibits human-like behavior.

Universities

In the 1950s, work began on the foundations of artificial intelligence. Carnegie Mellon University was the epicenter. Over the following three decades, AI research remained largely the business of universities, although IBM and the Bell Labs began to experiment. The development of AI during these decades was limited by the growing but still modest capabilities of computers.

The Tech Companies

As computer power accelerated during the last two decades of the 20th century, personal computers and then the internet begat major technology companies – Apple, Microsoft, Google, Facebook, Amazon and Alibaba. AI research and development migrated from the universities to these new technology giants. Much of the innovative university talent was bought up by these companies in a race to dominate the AI field. For example, in the late 1980s a team at Carnegie Mellon University developed a computer called *Deep Thought*, that challenged Garry Kasparov the world chess champion. Deep thought lost. But six years later, several people behind *Deep Thought* were at IBM where *Deep Thought* was re-invented as *Deep Blue* and beat Kasparov.

In 2014, Google acquired the London AI company DeepMind. The DeepMind subsidiary has set its sights on understanding how the human mind works as the foundation for progress toward full artificial intelligence. They currently employ over 250 PhDs.

The Broader Economy

As applications of AI have been proven to be economically viable, virtually every field has attracted entrepreneurs probing the potential for AI to replace human workers or extend human capabilities. AI is taking root from farming to medicine, manufacturing to lawyering, tax preparation, retail work, and law enforcement. Universities are preparing tens of thousands of students to be AI engineers. The tech companies are offering tools, some at no cost, to this flood of AI trained talent.

As illustrated in the chart below, all of this is coming to a head as computer power takes off with exponential growth.

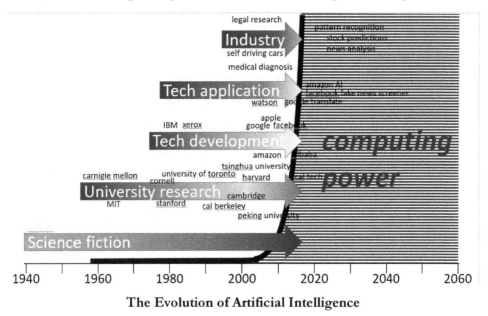

The Evolution of Artificial Intelligence

AI has spent the last sixty years in its infancy and adolescence. It has now graduated from school and is looking for work.

2. COMPUTERS VERSUS HUMANS

To come to our own conclusions about the future of AI, we need to assess the strengths and weaknesses of computers, where AI resides, and the strengths and weaknesses of the brain, where human intelligence resides. We must imagine how intelligence can emerge from seemingly unintelligent component parts.

Computer Hardware

The chart below gives a history of the computers that I have used since 1961.

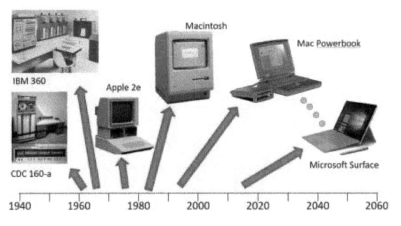

A Personal History of Computers

1961: The Control Data 160-A

In the summers of 1961 and 62, I worked at the National Security Agency and had a Control Data 160-A as my own personal computer. The desk in the picture is actually the computer. What looks like file drawers are actually the guts of the computer.

Control Data 160A

Random Access Memory (RAM)

In order to perform any kind of work, computers have to take information out of long term memory, such as the tape drive in the picture above, and bring it into its short-term memory or RAM, the place where actual computing gets done. The CDC 160A had about four thousand bytes of RAM. We need a few words at this point about bits and bytes.

Bits

At the most basic level, computer memory is represented as 1's and 0's, or binary digits called bits. Numbers are represented by 1's and 0's as shown in the table on the next page. As we count up, each time we get to all 1's we have to add another bit. In decimal counting, we can get up to nine with one digit, then we must go to two digits to represent the quantity 10. When we get to 99, we must add a third digit to get the quantity 100. Every time we get to the next power of ten, we have to add another digit. In binary counting we have to add digits far more frequently – every time we get to the next power of two. When we get to four, we have to add a third binary digit. When we get to sixty-four, we need a total of seven binary digits. With eight binary digits, we can count up to 255.

Decimal	Binary
0	0
1	1
2	10
3	11
4	100
...	
7	111
8	1000
...	
15	1111
16	10000
...	
31	11111
32	1000000
...	
63	111111
64	1000000
...	
127	1111111
128	10000000
...	
255	11111111
256	1000000000

Bytes

Computer memory is organized into groups of bits called bytes. Typically, there are eight bits per byte. You can count up to 255 in one eight-bit byte.

So back to my first personal computer, the Control Data 160A. It cost $800,000 in 2017 dollars. Therefore, its cost per kilobyte (thousand bytes) was about $195,000. Its calculation speed of 67,000 instructions per second sounds fast. These days, we are not used to worrying about the speed of our computers or ipads, since we are generally doing work that does not need a lot of calculation. But just for comparison, if you were to take iphone pictures with a computer running at the speed of the 160-A, it would take hours to store each picture.

Moore's Law

You may have heard of Moore's law. Gordon Moore was the founder of Intel, the computer chip maker. In 1975, he proclaimed that computer performance would double every two years for decades into the future.

To comprehend the implications of this rate of growth, there is the fable of the King of India and the chess board. At the annual "Gifts for the King" celebration, a lowly peasant presented the king a chess board and chess set. When he had taught the king how to play chess, the king was so pleased that he declared that the peasant could have any gift that he desired. The peasant said that his needs were modest. If the king could place one grain of rice in the first square of the chess board on the first day and then each of the next sixty-three days double the number of grains on each square, that would be sufficient.

On the 64th day, the gift of rice would cover the entire country of India – 1.25 million square miles at a depth of 5 inches.

1960s University Computers

In the 60s and 70s I did several projects on university computers. You would never actually see these computers, you would only interact through punch cards and reams of computer printouts passed back and forth through a narrow window like returning dishes in a cafeteria.

The IBM 360 was a typical university computer of the day. It cost about $1.7 million in today's dollars, with a RAM memory of 1 megabyte (one million bytes). This is a cost of $1,600 per kilobyte, down from the $200,000 of my first computer, and the speed had increased from 60,000 instructions per second to 16 million.

1978 The Apple IIe
Then, in 1978, the great breakthrough - the Apple IIe. In today's dollars, the IIe would cost $9,620 with RAM memory of 48,000 bytes. This reduced the cost per kilobyte to $200, one one-thousandth of the cost of my CDC 160-A. The IIe had a calculation speed of one million instructions per second.

1984 The Apple Macintosh
Six years later, the Apple Macintosh hit the streets with a cost per kilobyte of $45. It cost $5,752 in today's dollars with a memory of 128,000 bytes. Calculation speed was six times that of the Apple IIe.

1991 Mac Powerbook
At today's price of $8,226 and RAM memory of eight megabytes, the Powerbook cost per kilobyte was down to about $1.00. The Powerbook's speed was two and a half times the speed of the Macintosh.

Over the last twenty-five years, I have replaced my computer every two or three years to keep up with ever increasing performance.

2015 Microsoft Surface Pro

My current machine, the Microsoft Surface Pro, cost about $800. It has a RAM memory of four gigabytes (four billion bytes) resulting in a cost of $0.0002 per kilobyte or two ten thousandths of a dollar. It is running at 2.4 billion instructions per second.

So the average time to cut costs in half over the last 60 years has actually been about 22 months – under the two years predicted by Moore's Law.

Year	Computer	RAM kbytes	Cost (2017 $)	$/ kbyte	Ops per sec
1961	CDC 160-A	4	$800,000	$195,000	64,000
1968	IBM 360	1,000	$1.7 million	$1,600	16 million
1978	Apple IIe	48	$9,620	$200	1 million
1984	Macintosh	128	$5,752	$45	6 million
1991	Mac Powerbook	8,000	$8,226	$1.00	16 million
2015	Microsoft Surface	4,000,000	$800	$0.0002	2.4 billion

Computer Software

To appreciate the capabilities and limitations of computers we need a few words about the nature of computer software. Computer programs are step by step instructions that tell the computer what to do.

Some of us learned programming in the Fortran language developed for scientific calculation in the 1950s. Fortran is a classic language still in use today. There are many computer languages each with its own special syntax. The important thing to know is that computer programs are sequential, executing one step after another. The sample program below shows that the sequence of instructions can jump from one place to another using GOTO statements.

Fortran Program

```
10  READ(5,501) A,B,C
        IF(A.EQ.0 .AND. B.EQ.0 .AND. C.EQ.0) GO TO 50
        IF(A.EQ.0 .OR.  B.EQ.0 .OR.  C.EQ.0) GO TO 90
        S = (A + B + C) / 2.0
        AREA = SQRT( S * (S - A) * (S - B) * (S - C) )
        WRITE(6,601) A,B,C,AREA
        GO TO 10
50      WRITE(6,602)
        STOP
90      WRITE(6,603)
        STOP
        END
```

Sample FORTRAN Program

In this program, there are three GOTO statements. The one immediately following line 10 says: if the conditions within the IF statement are true, then go to line 50, otherwise proceed to the next line in sequence. The next line says go to line 90 if that IF statement is true. The third GOTO statement, just before line 50, takes us back to line 10 if the two IF statements allowed the program to proceed in sequence.

In sum, computers are fast, sequential, and accurate. But as we will see below, they are poor at pattern recognition.

Pattern Recognition

Pattern recognition is the understanding of the overall meaning of a collection of parts. Humans are fantastic pattern recognizers. For example, our brains have no problem seeing the overall pattern of a six in the next illustration.

18

Six easily recognized by the human brain

Because information comes into computers as a stream of 1's and 0's, discerning the overall meaning of a pattern is a challenge. Imagine trying to recognize this six if you had to look at one piece at a time.

Six in pieces – as a computer would see it

A classic test for a computer's ability to recognize patterns is a collection of hand written numbers. We humans have no trouble recognizing these numbers, maybe with a few exceptions. But why are we so good at it?

Sample of Hand Written Numbers

In essence, we swallow images whole. We have about a million nerve channels connecting our eyes to our cerebral cortex.

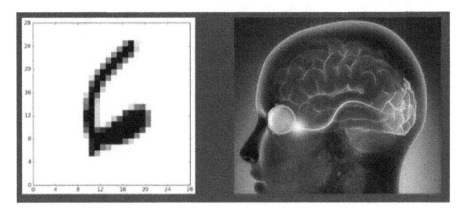

The signals generated by the eye come charging through a massively parallel network of neurons as shown below. The neurons are highly interconnected with one another.

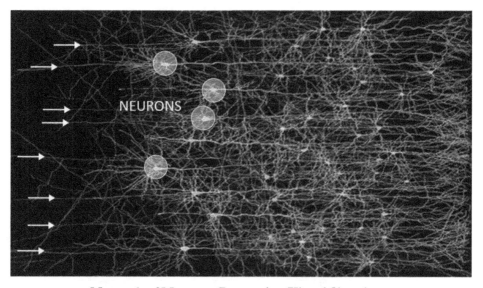

Network of Neurons Processing Visual Signals

Each neuron has thousands of incoming connections called dendrites. When the neuron fires off a signal it connects through its axon the thousands of downstream neurons.

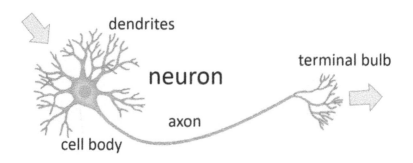

As shown in the picture below, neurons are connected through synapses. The strength of these connecting synapses determines if the incoming signals are strong enough to cause the downstream neuron to fire. Our memory is captured by the strength of synapses. Neurons in the human neo-cortex average about 10,000 connections to other neurons downstream.

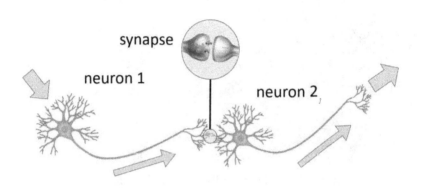

Synaptic connection between neurons

There are about 300 trillion synapses in the neocortex, 1000 trillion in the human brain as a whole. Each one is a memory unit. It retains properties that amplify or dampen signals coming from one neuron to the next. Synapses can retain their strength property indefinitely allowing us to remember events of our childhood.

The following drawing is a dramatically simplified illustration of how we see the number 6. I am showing forty-nine signals coming from the eye rather than a million. These signals are connected to several layers of neurons. The layers are densely interconnected by synapses. The last inner layer of neurons is connected to neurons that represent numbers.

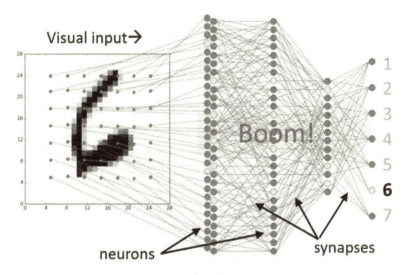

Neural Network Connects Image to Concept Neuron

Because the synapses that tie the neurons together vary in strength, the pattern represented by the number 6 is connected through directly to the conceptual 6 neuron. The BOOM! is meant to indicate that this happens in a hurry. There is no thinking involved.

A different number 6 will stimulate a slightly different set of neurons in the first layer, but ultimately be connected to the same conceptual 6 neuron. The generalized pattern for six is captured in the strengths of the synapses that tie this neural network together.

We were not born recognizing the number 6. The process of learning what is a six involves calibrating the strength of the synapses connecting the brains neuron that represents six to the various visual patterns that we learn to be sixes. This is how we learn everthing.

When you look at the picture on the next page, what do you see? Just as with the number 6, you process this more complex image almost immediately, even though it is rather odd, what with the magic carpet. If you cover the shadow of the flag, the carpet settles back down onto the sand. We have thousands of neural networks in our brain that make sense of incoming images, as well as incoming sounds, smells, tastes and touch sensations.

Illusion created by the shadow of a flag

Computers versus Humans

Now let's compare the strengths and weaknesses of computers and humans.

Capacity: Random Access Memory

The largest computers are now at 100 billion bytes and growing year by year. The human neocortex has about 30 billion neurons, but the synapses, where learning really occurs, number about 300 trillion.

Operating Speed

Operating speed is not much of a contest with computers now at billions of operations per second and the brain at about 100 (not 100 billion, just 100, the number that follows 99).

Simultaneous Operations

Computer operation is sequential with one thread of calculations while the brain fires off millions and perhaps billions of interconnected operations at a time. It is true that for some problems, computer processors have been set up to operate in parallel. To do this, the problem they are working on must be broken up into parts with each part assigned to a separate computer processor. This is quite different from neural networks (the brain) where simultaneous processes extensively interact with each other. Computer chips are under development to support neuron-like simultaneous interactions.

Operation

Computers run rule based programs. The human brain learns, recognizes, predicts and executes patterns. These ways of operating reflect the sequential nature of computer programs, and the brain's ability to process entire patterns.

To summarize:

Computers are sequential; the brain is parallel.
Computers are fast; the brain is slow.
Computers struggle with pattern recognition; for the brain, patterns are natural.
Computers are accurate; the brain is approximate.

3. EMERGENCE

How does human intelligence emerge from this seeming quagmire of neurons with their thousands of connecting synapses? The concept of **emergence** is used in science to refer to systems where relatively simple parts produces unexpected and sometimes extraordinary behavior.

Oren Etzioni of the Allen Institute for AI offers this observation: *Intelligence never looks like much when you look under the hood.*

The Moon and the Earth

A simple example of emergence can be found in the behavior of the Moon and the Earth.

Most of my life, I have been satisfied with my understanding of the relationship between the Moon and the Earth.

One day, several years ago, I was playing with an upgraded computer simulation program. This new version of the software had the cool feature of allowing me to move objects around on a worksheet using computer programs. To get familiar with how this worked, I created objects to represent celestial bodies – Earth, Moon, etc. Each object could be endowed with a mass and an initial velocity. I then wrote a program to simulate the gravitational pull of each object on all of the other objects on the worksheet. To test the program, I looked up the mass of the Earth and the Moon as well as the velocity of the Moon in its orbit around the Earth.

I put the Earth in the middle of the worksheet and put the Moon the proper distance from the Earth. If I had gotten all of these numbers right, and if I had the right formula for gravitational attraction, the Moon should move around the Earth in about twenty-seven simulated days.

The diagram of the Earth/Moon system shown below represents the way I visualized the system behaving. The Moon rotates in a circular (or perhaps slightly elliptical) orbit with the center of the orbit being at the center of the Earth.

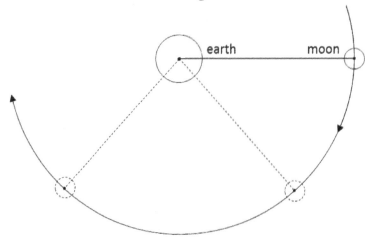

Mistaken View of Earth-Moon System (not to scale)

After a bit of debugging, my little Moon, about the size of a pencil eraser, moved slowly around my dime-sized Earth. As I stared at the screen admiring my work, I thought I detected a slight wobble in the Earth icon. I zoomed the screen, and the wobble was quite clear. The Earth was wobbling one revolution for each revolution of the Moon around the Earth. Was this real or was it an anomaly of my model?

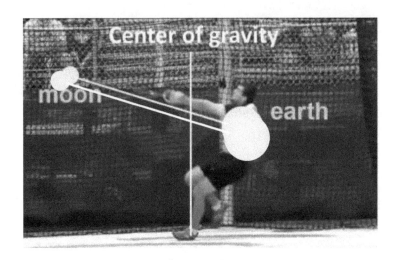

Olympic hammer throw like Earth and Moon

Think of the hammer-throw event in the Olympics. A three-hundred-pound man throws a sixteen-pound ball at the end of a four-foot cable. He does this by spinning three or four times with the hammer whizzing around him. If you can picture this, the man is leaning backward with his heels braced into the ground. We can look at the man and the hammer as a system that is rotating around a point in front of the man's chest. The man and the ball are circling this point. Think of the Moon as the hammer and the Earth as the man.

Join me in one more analogy. If you think of a cheerleader's baton tossed in the air, it rotates around its center. The two weights on the ends of the baton are equal. If you made a baton where one end weighs ten times more than the other, the baton would rotate around a point close to the end with the larger weight. The Earth has about eighty times the mass of the Moon. The Earth-Moon *baton* rotates around a point that is about one-eightieth of the distance between the center of the Earth and the center of the Moon. Since the two bodies are about 235,000 miles apart, this point is about

2,900 miles from the Earth end of the baton, or about 1,100 miles below the surface of the Earth. Bottom line, every twenty-seven days or so the Earth wobbles around a point about 2,900 miles from its center.

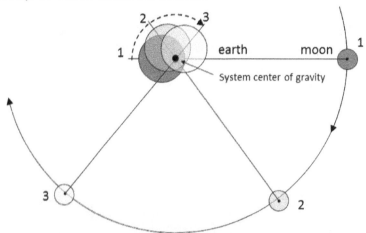

Earth-Moon System Rotates Around its Center of Gravity

In the figure above, the Earth and Moon rotate around the point indicated as the *system center of gravity*. As the Moon moves from position one to position two to position three, the Earth also moves through positions one, two, and three. Every twenty-seven days, the Earth wobbles around the system's center of gravity.

What we take to be obvious properties of even simple systems may be quite different for what emerges from the interaction of their parts.

Starlings

The balletic movement of flocks of starlings, called murmurations, emergences from behavioral rules that dictate how each bird flies in relation to its neighbors. When a flock of starlings perceives danger, it flies in amazing formations without any obvious coordination mechanism, as shown in the following image.[2]

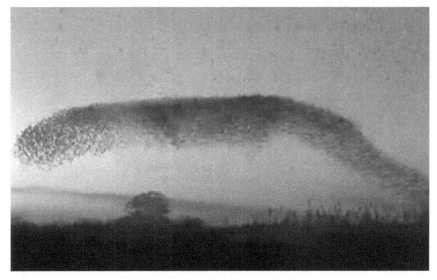

Murmeration of Starlings

Emergence of Human Intelligence

So how does human intelligence emerge from a collection of neurons and synapses, however complex that collection may be? We will be exploring this question, but I would like to introduce you to two authors who have gotten me thinking on this subject over the years: Marvin Minsky and Jeff Hawkins.

---

[2] See a marvelous video by googling *murmurations video.*

Marvin Minsky

In 1974, Marvin Minsky, the long-time head of the Artificial Intelligence lab at MIT, proposed *Frame Theory*[3] to explain how the brain works. He argued that the building blocks of cognition are not minute and unstructured elements, but rather more elaborate data structures that model the systems we are thinking about. He calls these structures frames. We have a lightning-fast ability to match situations we encounter with one of the thousands of frames we have in our mental filing system. With each new problem we encounter, the frame we call up guides us in collecting information to build a situation-specific mental model. These models provide an explanation of the dynamics of a situation and allow us to predict the outcomes of alternative courses of action.

He explains his theory as follows:

> *Here is the essence of the theory: when one encounters a new situation (or makes a substantial change in one's view of the present situation), one selects from memory a structure called a Frame. This is a remembered framework to be adapted to fit reality by changing details as necessary.*
>
> *A frame is a data-structure for representing a stereotyped situation, like being in a certain kind of*

---

[3] *A Framework for Representing Knowledge*, Artificial Intelligence Memo No 306, Massachusetts Institute of Technology, Artificial Intelligence Laboratory, 1974.

living room, or going to a child's birthday party. At-
tached to each frame are several kinds of
information. Some of this information is about how to
use the frame. Some is about what one can expect to
happen next. Some is about what to do if these expec-
tations are not confirmed.

Minsky further refined his thinking in the 1985 book *So-ciety of Mind*.[4] In his introduction, he summarized as follows:

This book tries to explain how minds work. How can intelligence emerge from nonintelligence? To an-swer that, we'll show that you can build a mind from many little parts, each mindless by itself.

I'll call "Society of Mind" this scheme in which each mind is made of many smaller processes. These we'll call agents. Each mental agent by itself can only do some simple thing that needs no mind or thought at all. Yet when we join these agents in societies-in certain very special ways-this leads to true intelli-gence.

Jeff Hawkins

In his book *On Intelligence*,[5] Jeff Hawkins puts prediction at the center of human intelligence. The following story serves as an illustration.

Our family has vacationed for generations on the eastern shore of Delaware where eating crabs is a religion. One day my four-year-old granddaughter asked me to describe how to

---

[4] *Society of Mind*, Simon and Schuster, New York. 1985.
[5] *On Intelligence*, Henry Holt and Company, New York. 2004.

catch a crab. I explained that you go out on a dock, or maybe in a boat, where you think there might be crabs in the water. You tie a piece of meat - I thought *chicken neck* would seem gross - to a string and lower it into the water. You hold the string lightly in your hand, and when you feel the string wiggling, it means that there may be one or two crabs nibbling at the meat. Slowly, you pull the string up until you can see if a crab is there. You bring the crab near the surface of the water. Then you take your net, slip it into the water, and swoop it up from under the crab.

Nora declared, "Then you have to put a lid on the net." In an instant, she had visualized the crab climbing out of the net. She had never seen a live crab. Yet she effortlessly created this scene in her mind and played it forward, predicting what the crab would do, and what to do about it.

According to Jeff Hawkins, this ability of the human mind to predict what will happen next is at the heart of human intelligence. Hawkins made a fortune as the developer of the Palm Pilot. He has dedicated his post-Palm Pilot years to investigating how the mind works. His seminal work, On Intelligence, presents his model of the functioning of the neocortex, the part of the brain that makes mammals so special, and humans more special yet. His core idea is that the neocortex is made up of invariant representations of all aspects of the world that we experience. These representations are generalized. Hawkins notion of representations is comparable to Minsky's idea of frames.

For example, we remember a person's face as a single model, not as a particular view or combination of views. We are able, in ways not fully understood, to use this model not only to recognize a person from various views but also from partial views and from views we have never seen before. Our memory is filled with these representations. In fact, our memory is these representations. We use them continuously to predict what will happen next. When what happens does not match our prediction, the difference gets our attention. For Hawkins, prediction and action are closely linked. According to Hawkins, Nora's visualization of the crab climbing out of the net is what the most recently developed components of the brain are designed to do – predict what is going to happen next.

> *The brain uses vast amounts of memory to create a model of the world. Everything you know and have learned is stored in this model. The brain uses this memory-based model to make continuous predictions of future events. It is the ability to make predictions about the future that is the crux of intelligence.*[6]

After publication of *On Intelligence*, Hawkins founded Numenta, a tech firm dedicated to developing artificial intelligence algorithms closely modeled after what is known about neural functioning in the neocortex. The Numenta AI system is called HTM (Hierarchical Temporal Memory). Numenta is committed to sharing their approach.[7]

---

[6] Hawkins, *On Intelligence*, p. 6.
[7] See Google "HTM School" for access to a series of You Tube videos explaining their approach.

Frames and Invariant Representations are Pattern Recognizers

The frames of Marvin Minsky and the Invariant Representations of Jeff Hawkins are pattern recognizers. The configuration of neurons and synapses that recognize the number six is a frame. Frames (I'll use that term since it is shorter than *invariant representations*) not only recognize patterns, but also fill in missing details, predict the behavior of the system being recognized and may have associated actions based on those predictions. Of course, the number 6 is not a very dynamic pattern but consider the images below[8]. Not only do you recognize these as bicycles but also may imagine the irregular ride that they would provide.

Irregular bicycles

---

[8] Adapted from Edward de Bono, *The Mechanism of Mind*, (New York: Penguin Books, 1969) p. 150.

4. THE QUESTION

Should machine intelligence try to duplicate the mechanisms of human intelligence?

This is not a new question. While I was in architecture school in 1965, I took a course from Brad Dunham on design by natural selection. Brad was an engineer at IBM who used his design ideas to develop the logic of the IBM 360 computer. I thought that maybe his approach could be applied to architecture.

The final exam in that course had the following question:

> *It is an old saw in the domain of "artificial intelligence" problems that one should base one's approach on the way in which people themselves solve such problems. To what extent is that old saw correct?*

Quite remarkable that in 1965 we were talking about "old saws" of artificial intelligence.

Since the 1950s there have been two theories of AI that answer yes to this question. Rule-based AI tries to emulate the logical functioning of human intelligence. Neuron-based AI tries to model the neural network that captures patterns of human experience.

In the 1950s Herbert Simon started the ball rolling on rule-based AI, while Frank Rosenblatt pursued the neuron-based approach.

Rule-Based AI

Herbert Simon was an economist who dedicated himself to understanding human problem solving. In the 1950s and 60s, he and Allen Newell at Carnegie Mellon University tirelessly studied how graduate students solved various kinds of puzzles. This resulted in the landmark book *Human Problem Solving*,[9] and led to the development of rule-based artificial intelligence.

The basic principle of rule-based AI was to capture knowledge about how to do things in the form of IF . . . THEN statements. Sets of these statements in subject areas like medicine and engineering became known as EXPERT SYSTEMS.

In the 1970s expectations for expert systems grew, with substantial research and development funding from the US military largely through The Defense Advanced Research Projects Agency (DARPA). As these systems moved out of the universities into the real world they grew in complexity and proved to be unwieldy. By the late 1980s enthusiasm had subsided.

In 1989, a team at Carnegie Mellon attempted to challenge the world chess champion Gary Kasparov to a match

---

[9] Allen Newell and Herbert Simon, *Human Problem Solving*. Englewood Cliffs, New Jersey, Prentiss-Hall, 1972.

with a rule-based AI system. Failure ensued. IBM took over the Carnegie Mellon effort and dubbed it Deep Blue. After failing to beat Kasparov in 1994, Deep Blue finally succeeded in 1995 bringing substantial publicity to AI during a period when it had been long considered over-hyped.

Watson

Then IBM's Watson came along. Named after IBM's founder, Watson is a complex set of rule-based AI algorithms that answers questions in specific subject areas.

In 2007, engineers at IBM took on the challenge of developing Watson to the point where it could defeat the all-time champion of the TV quiz show Jeopardy. Their assessment in 2007 was that the best AI programs could get about 15% of the Jeopardy questions right. The chart below shows that Ken Jennings was at about 95%.

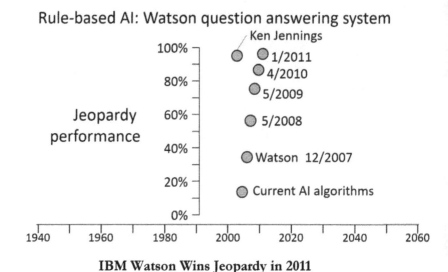

IBM Watson Wins Jeopardy in 2011

In December of 2007, the first version of Watson adapted to the Jeopardy format produced 35% correct answers.[10] Hard work over three years was required to get Watson to the point where it could compete with Jennings.

The Watson approach has two parts. First, it scanned a broad knowledge base and converted it into a standardized vocabulary and sentence structure. Second, it converted each question into a standard sentence structure so it could be matched with sentences in the knowledge base.

If you Google the phrase "dog bites man" the first references that are returned are about men biting dogs. In this case, Google ignores the syntax of "dog bites man" in favor of the popularity of certain stories that include the words dog, bite, and man in no particular order. Watson pays attention to word order in the way that it organizes reference material and in the way in analyzes questions. In the example shown on the next page, the newspaper headline is converted into a standard form that can be quickly matched with questions expressed in the same language.

---

[10] Technically they were correct questions since the Jeopardy game format was to provide an answer with the contestants coming up with an appropriate question.

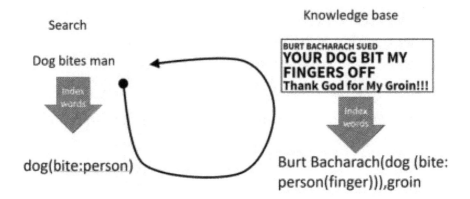

Knowledge Base Search Using Structured Language

5. NEURON-BASED AI

How Machines Learn

Computers can learn by altering their memory based on experience. A computer's experience can be internally generated, as in playing games against itself, or externally generated by comparing the results of its actions against a set of goals.

In 1982, the movie War Games featured a super-computer, WOPR, that went out of control. While WOPR was about to start World War III, our hero Matthew Broderick set the computer to playing tic tac toe against itself in the hopes that it would learn the futility of playing a game that it could not win. When asked by his girlfriend "what is it doing", he proclaimed "it's learning." The gambit succeeded as WOPR tried one WWIII strategy after another without finding a winning approach. It finally declared "why play a game where neither side can win?"

Design by Natural Selection

Back to the aforementioned professor Brad Dunham. He was a computer designer at IBM. In 1961, when analytical methods at IBM were failing to come up with an optimal design for the circuits of the IBM 360, he developed an innovate way for computers to *learn* a good design, a trial and error approach he called natural selection. The method seems simple. You start with any design at all, and try a small random change. If the change makes the design better, you keep it; if not, you reject it. You continue with the process until there is no more improvement. To do this, you must have a way to score each design to determine if you have an improvement. As with most things in life, the process is not as simple as it sounds, but with embellishments it worked for Brad and resulted in the design of the 360 circuitry.

I applied Brad's methods to a simple architectural design problem where the elements of the design to varying degrees "wanted" to be near each other. The design started with parts of certain zones together, but the elements as a whole spread out, as shown in the first frame of the illustration on the next page. The initial score was 3,812, a measure of the distance between the elements that wanted to be together. The goal of the process was to make this score as low as possible, indicating that things wanting to be close together were satisfied. Every time there were 20 improvements in the design, I recorded the layout as shown on the next page.

It took seventy-one random attempts to make the first twenty improvements as shown in the second frame of the illustration. At this point, the score has been lowered from 3,812 to 3,121. It took another 346 random tries to get the next twenty improvements, bringing the score down to 2,003.

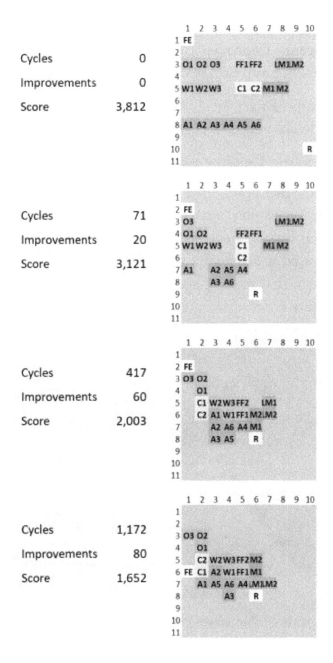

Cycles	0
Improvements	0
Score	3,812

Cycles	71
Improvements	20
Score	3,121

Cycles	417
Improvements	60
Score	2,003

Cycles	1,172
Improvements	80
Score	1,652

Floor Plan Layout by Natural Selection

43

Finally, an additional 755 random attempts resulted in the last twenty improvements. There were no further improvements in a run of 5,000 cycles.

At a rudimentary level, this is how computers can learn and actually is often how humans learn – by trial and error.

Space Antenna Designed by Natural Selection

In 1995, five competing contractors failed to design an antenna for a satellite that met NASA specifications. They used various human analytical methods. Jason Lohn, a NASA engineer, used a design by natural selection to evolve this quirky design that met the specifications and was a huge success in practice.

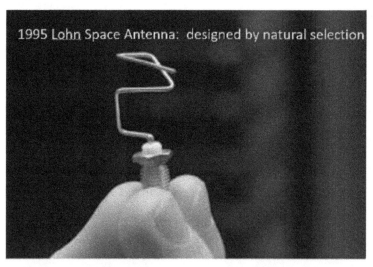

1995 Lohn Space Antenna: designed by natural selection

Jason Lohn's space antenna

Development of Neuron-Based AI Systems

Neuron-based AI systems are learning machines. Their capabilities are not programmed; they are learned.

The following appeared in the New York Times:

Perceptrons will be able to recognize people and call out their names. Printed pages, longhand letters and even speech commands are within their reach. Only one more step of development, a difficult step, is needed for the device to hear speech in one language and instantly translate it to speech or writing in another language.

These were the words of Frank Rosenblatt in 1958.

Since he lacked a computer that could meet his needs, Rosenblatt constructed the Perceptron himself to model the way that our neural networks process incoming information. In the sketch below, he showed three neural layers: the input, a hidden layer, and the output. It was designed to be a pattern recognizer.

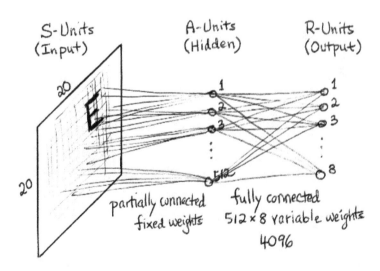

Sketch of the perceptron by Frank Rosenblatt

Throughout the 1960s, advocates of rule-based AI ridiculed Rosenblatt's work. In 1969, Marvin Minsky, published a book that "proved" that the perceptron theory was bunk.

Two years later Rosenblatt died in a car crash, and his work died with him.

In the early eighties, John Hopfield of Bell Labs, took up the work that Rosenblatt had started, developing multi-layer networks with a variety of connectivity patterns.

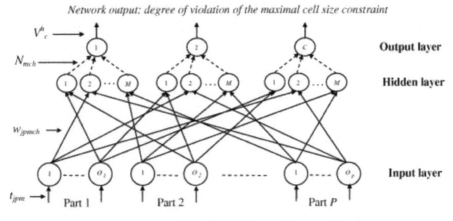

Hopfield Network

Around that time, Geoff Hinton developed learning methods for neuron-based AI that significantly increased their viability. Hinton got his PhD in AI from the University of Edinburgh. A Canadian by birth, he held positions at universities in England, Canada, and the US, notably at Carnegie Mellon in Pittsburg. This was at a time when excitement over rule-based AI was on the wane. His new AI learning method was called BACK-PROPAGATION.

Back-Propagation

So how does a computer learn to recognize a dog?

Let's start with the fact that a computer "sees" an image as an array of pixels. Obviously the seven-by-seven grid in the illustration below is a simplification.

The image pixels are connected to an input layer of "neurons" modeled in the computer. These are then connected through "synapses" and several layers of neurons back to neurons that represent classes of objects. Before the network has learned to recognize dogs, the network randomly connects images to concepts, and may light up dog, cat, and other object neurons.

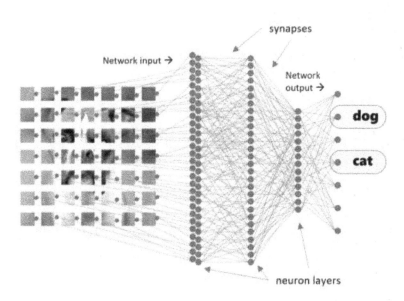

Untrained network yet to learn what a dog is

We now tell the network that this is a dog. This is called supervised training. The neural network then strengthens the synapses connecting this image to DOG, and weakens the synapses connecting other concepts to the dog image. This process is called BACK PROPAGATION. (See illustration below.)

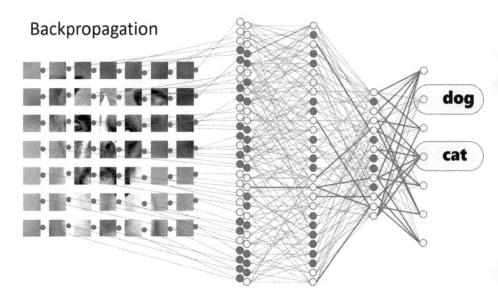

Backpropagation

Backpropagation strengthens connections between image and concept of dog (heavy lines indicate blocked channels)

To train the network to recognize dogs, we would show it dog pictures from different angles, each time telling it that this is a dog. We would show many breeds of dog. Again, we would strengthen the synapses leading to dog and weaken those leading to other concepts. Eventually the strengths of the synapses in this network capture a general concept of DOGNESS, of what it means to look like a DOG. We can then train the network on cats.

Microsoft On-line Image Recognition

Image recognition software is now widely available for many applications. Microsoft has a web site where you can submit a picture and it will try to describe what it sees. I showed it this picture of my grandson playing tennis and it replied: "Young man hitting a tennis ball" with a probability of 83%.

Image recognition by Microsoft Cognitive Services

Then I tried the more difficult picture from Cambodia shown on the next page. It was described as a giraffe standing next to a tree in front of a stone wall. Confidence: 3.6%.

A giraffe standing next to a tree in front of a stone wall

How Learning Works in Humans

In the neuron-based AI training process, the AI must be told what the object is in order for backpropagation to strengthen the appropriate synapses. Humans can also learn what a thing is by being told: "this is a dog." In humans, being told that a thing is a dog invokes a conscious process which can then trigger the human equivalent of backpropagation[11]. If a human brain sees a thing it does not recognize, it could ask someone what it is. Or it could consciously investigate, looking for clues in order to identify what it is, then invoke the strengthening of appropriate synapses.

My rumination is that humans commonly learn a thing consciously and then learning is gradually transferred to the

_____

[11] Neuroscience has not yet explained how the human equivalent of backpropagation works.

subconscious synaptic structure. Learning sports skills by being told what to do or watching others perform a skill can result in a conscious understanding of the skill. However, often, the conscious mind cannot keep pace with the demands of the skill and the learner performs badly. Performance improves as the skill migrates to the neural network that processes incoming information and triggers appropriate responses subconsciously.

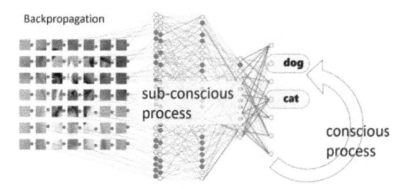

Learning migrates from conscious to subconscious processes

6. LEARNING SEQUENCES

So far, we have only been looking at recognizing two dimensional visual patterns - pictures. This by no means represent the full extent of human intelligence, but it's a start. I would argue that these networks know the meaning of the things they are recognizing, certainly more so than Google when you search the word DOG and it delivers sites that feature a word with the letters D-O-G. Being able to recognize a boy playing tennis would enable an AI to extend its understanding of what a boy is.

Jeff Hawkins built his model of human intelligence on the central role of learning sequences. By knowing the sequence in which things happen, we are able to predict what is coming next, based on what we have observed so far. For Hawkins, human behavior is a constant process of predicting what is about to happen and acting on the basis of this flow of predictions.

Verbal Prediction

What about patterns over time like music, stories, driving a car, or a sequence of actions? We remember sequences in one direction, from beginning to end. We are constantly predicting what is going to come next.

Given the following lines, we predict the lines to come without really trying.

> *My country 'tis of thee,*
> *Sweet land of liberty,*

But given the words of the song in reverse, it is difficult to recite it from end to beginning. What is the next word when we move from the end toward the beginning?

> *.Sing I thee of*

Sequences of words, music, and actions are strongly strung together from beginning to end but have no links tying them together from end to beginning.

Machine Translation

Demis Hassabis is a bright young Englishman who has made a huge impact on neuron-based AI. He co-founded the company DeepMind in London in 2010. Google acquired DeepMind in 2014 and now they have put over 250 PhD's to work. DeepMind has been applying neuron-based AI in a number of areas. Let's start with language translation.

In 2006, Google started developing Google Translate, a free service that translates among over 100 languages. Until late 2016, it used rule-based AI methods with mixed results. During 2016, Hassibis convinced the Google Translate team to abandon ten years of development and switch over to a neuron-based AI scheme. Rather than using English as a stepping stone between languages, the neuron-based approach goes directly between language pairs. The new scheme learned its translation skills from millions of translated sentences available through the UN and other translation services.

To test the impact of the new neuron-based translator, Jun Rekimoto, a distinguished professor of human-computer interaction at the University of Tokyo, translated this bit of Hemmingway into Japanese.

Kilimanjaro is a snow-covered mountain 19,710 feet high, and is said to be the highest mountain in Africa. Its western summit is called the Masai "Ngaje Ngai," the House of God. Close to the western summit there is the dried and frozen carcass of a leopard. No one has explained what the leopard was seeking at that altitude.

He then used the Google's old rule-based AI and the new neuron-based AI to translate it back to English as shown in the tables below.

Original	Kilimanjaro is a snow-covered mountain 19,710 feet high, and is said to be the highest mountain in Africa.
Japanese	キリマンジャロは 19,710 フィートの高さの雪で覆われた山で、アフリカで最も高い山と言われています。
Rule-based	Kilimanjaro is 19,710 feet of the mountain covered with snow, and it is said that the highest mountain in Africa.
Neuron-based	Kilimanjaro is a mountain of 19,710 feet covered with snow and is said to be the highest mountain in Africa.

Translation of the First Sentence

Original	No one has explained what the leopard was seeking at that altitude.
Japanese	ヒョウがその標高で探していたものは誰も説明していません。
Rule-based	Whether the leopard had what the demand at that altitude, there is no that nobody explained.
Neuron-based	No one has ever explained what leopard wanted at that altitude.

Translation of the Last Sentence

It is clear from these examples that the neuron-based translation system resulted in far clearer and more fluid sentences.

I did an experiment of my own using the current neuron-based translator.[12] I translated a simple sentence from English to Japanese and then back to English. I think the English might have been improved. See the results below.

---

[12] To use the current version of Google Translate, type "translate" into the Google search box and the translation tool will pop up.

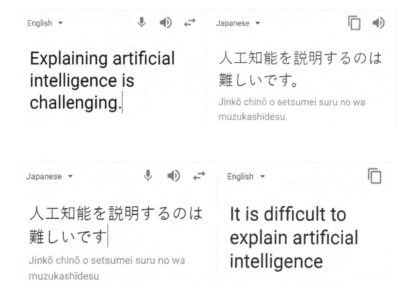

English ▼   🎤 🔊 ⇄

Explaining artificial intelligence is challenging.

Japanese ▼   📋 🔊

人工知能を説明するのは難しいです。

Jinkō chinō o setsumei suru no wa muzukashīdesu.

Japanese ▼   🎤 🔊 ⇄

人工知能を説明するのは難しいです

Jinkō chinō o setsumei suru no wa muzukashīdesu

English ▼   📋

It is difficult to explain artificial intelligence

Translation from English to Japanese and Back to English

7. LEARNING ACTIONS

So far, we have looked at AI understanding of visual patterns and sequential patterns, but what about action? Answering a question or translating Hemmingway could be considered actions, but what about actions like driving a car?

Most actions we take are instinctive, subconscious, like driving a car while we think about something else. Other actions are the result of careful planning. In either case, our actions are based on our prediction that the actions we take will result in a good outcome. In a given situation, we take action X to get result Y. We could consider making moves in a game like chess to be actions, but this seems to be missing the dynamic nature of day-to-day life.

Reaction Time

One easily overlooked feature of human action is the delay that occurs between the information we receive through our senses and the actions we are able to take in response. This delay time is between 0.2 to 0.4 seconds, depending on the complexity of the action. This is significant because it requires that we base our moment to moment actions on the state of affairs we predict will prevail a short time in the future.

Let's look at the actions of Roger Federer. You might think that he is just doing "see ball – hit ball." But actually, he has to predict where the ball is going to be in the near-term future.

In the illustration below, I have frozen the action with the ball about two tenths of a second away from Federer's racquet. Because even the best athletes need about three tenths of a second to process visual information and take an action, anything he sees between now and when he hits the ball cannot help him to know where the ball will be. This picture shows an image of the racquet head in the position where he will actually hit the ball. He must be able to predict that point of contact now, since he will get no further information that he can use.

Roger Federer reacting to on coming ball

How does he know where that point is? He has learned to read the flight of the ball, perhaps including the sound of his opponents hit and the spin of the ball. But this is not a calculation. It is a pattern that he reads instinctively. It is embedded in his neural network. Boom!

Atari

Demis Hassibis of DeepMind has been obsessed with Atari games. He wants to prove that his neuron-based AI can play them all better that the best human players.

Atari, Inc. dominated the video game industry during the 1970s and 1980s for both commercial arcades and home computers. The Atari game called BREAKOUT is shown in the picture below.

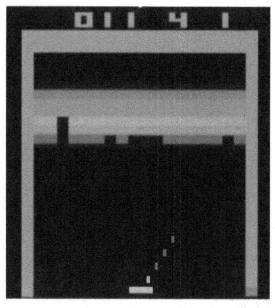

Atari game Breakout first released in 1978

The player moves a paddle at the bottom of the screen to bounce the ball up against a wall of bricks, trying to break through it.

Mastering this game was an early accomplishment of DeepMind's neuron-based AI systems. To play the game, the AI is fed only the pixels on the screen. Its only goal is to get the best score (shown on the upper left). Its only actions are to move the paddle left or right. It learns to play by a process called reinforcement learning in which it determines what actions lead ultimately to improvements in the score.

At first, the AI plays the game with no skill at all. After about 400 training sessions, it plays with the skill of an advanced player. After 600 sessions, it plays at the level of the most advanced expert.

Hassibis has applied the same AI design to all of the Atari games of the 1980s and outperformed humans on all but two. Reinforcement learning is much like the work of behaviorists, Pavlov and Skinner, who trained dogs and pigeons.

Each point in time during the game, the AI is looking at the last four images shown on the next page. From this, it can predict where the ball is going and when it will get there. The AI learns to match this prediction with the action of moving the paddle to the right place in order to redirect the ball and improve the game score.

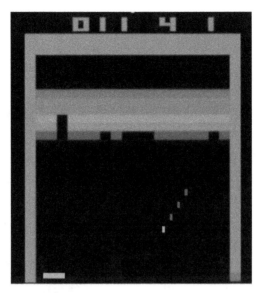

AI playing Breakout remembers the last four time steps

Atari's Space Wars presenteded a much more difficult challenge since it has more moving parts. It took several years for DeepMind to overtake the best human gamers in the more advanced Atari games.

Self-Driving Cars

ALVINN was the first self-driving car. It navigated its way around the Carnegie Mellon University campus in 1995. ALVINN was only responsible for steering not accelerating and braking. To train ALVINN, a human drove along a stretch of road while the ALVINN system learned and updated the weights of the synapses in its neuron-based AI. By the end of that time, the driver could let go of the wheel and the system would continue driving on an entirely new stretch of road.[13]

The DARPA Grand Challenge

In 2004, DARPA[14] initiated the Grand Challenge event. DARPA offered a one million dollar prize to the driverless vehicle that could complete a 150-mile off-road course in the shortest time. Of the more than one hundred teams that entered the competition, Carnegie Mellon's entry showed the most endurance, completing seven miles of the course. No prize was awarded.

In 2005 the prize was upped to two million dollars. Five vehicles completed the course. The entry from the Stanford Artificial Intelligence Lab finished first followed by two entries from Carnegie Mellon.

In 2007, DARPA's Urban Challenge attracted attention from all over the world. Initial entries were whittled down to eleven finalists. In several cases, university research groups teamed up with manufacturers including GM, Volkswagen, and Oshkosh Truck. The team from Carnegie Mellon and GM won the competition.

Since that time, most major car makers have committed to developing autonomous cars. Elements of computer

---

[13] See https://www.youtube.com/watch?v=ilP4aPDTBPE for a video on the ALVINN project.

[14] DARPA is the Defense Advanced Research Projects Agency, the most prominent research organization of the United States Department of Defense.

driver assistance have become standard equipment on most new cars, including lane detection, control of following distance, and in some models, crash avoidance.

Tesla has led the way in making fully autonomous operation available commercially. Since 2015, Tesla cars have been equipped with self-driving features that can operate on limited access highways. When the car detects that it is on a road for which it is not qualified, it informs the human driver to take over control.

A good overview of the state of the art as of mid 2017 is available on a You Tube video. Search for "Google self-driving video" to find the video.

8. Engineering Artificial Intelligence

If you were taking MIT's on-line course on self-driving cars, you would be challenged to modify the program shown below[15] to get the maximum speed through heavy traffic.[16] I can report that I got a passing grade but did not challenge the top students.

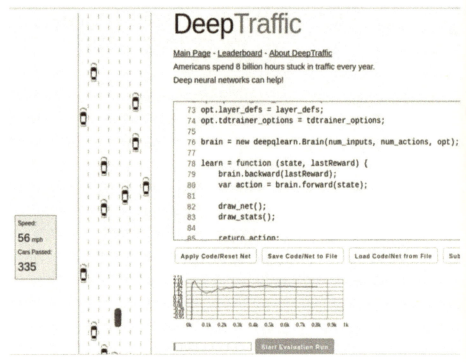

MIT Deep Traffic Web Site

---

[15] The program is in the window with the line numbers.

[16] See the following web site: http://selfdrivingcars.mit.edu/deep-trafficjs/

The Basics of Neural Network Design

AI engineering students are learning to put together the components of deep neural networks much as structural engineers learn to put together building structures. They must prepare themselves to be lifelong learners since the techniques of construction are being constantly expanded and refined.

Neuron-based AI systems are built from layers of neurons interconnected through synapses that are trained to perform various functions. A simple one-layer network designed to recognize individual numbers starts with a 28 x 28 grid of 784 pixels (shown in the illustration below). These 784 pixels are fully interconnected with 10 output neurons requiring 7840 synapses. After being trained on thousands of samples, this network is capable of about 90% accuracy in recognizing hand-written numbers.

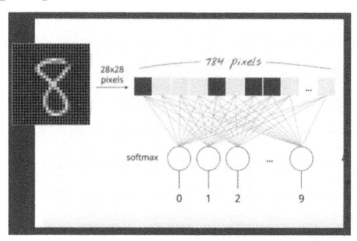

One Layer Fully Connected Neural Network

A neural network of five layers as shown below can recognize numbers with about 98% accuracy.

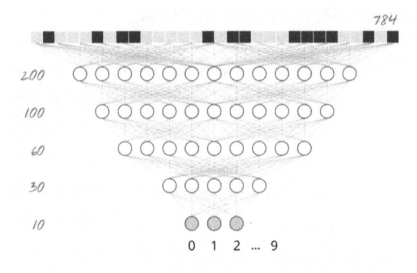

Fiv- Layer Fully Connected Neural Network

A more complex network with three convolutional layers can achieve over 99% accuracy, which is about a human level of accuracy. Convolutional layers map groups of neurons from one layer to single neurons on the next layer. This has the effect of preserving the spatial relationships among neurons to some extent.

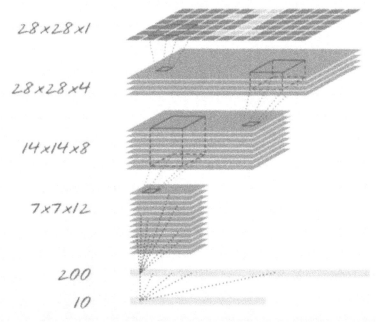

28×28×1

28×28×4

14×14×8

7×7×12

200

10

Five-Layer Network with Three Convolutional Layers

Over the last thirty years, many techniques have been developed for engineering neural networks for various purposes starting with the work of Rosenblatt, Hopfield, and Hinton. The next illustration shows a nine-layer network combining convolutional and fully connected layers. This network was designed for picture classification. Networks have been built with as many as one hundred layers.

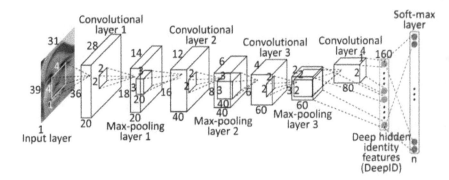

Example of complex deep neural network

Programming Neural Networks

AI students are learning how to design and program these complex neural networks. Programs like TensorFlow, developed by Google, make specification of these networks relatively simple once they are designed. Each layer in the network requires just one or two lines of code.

```
36    # specify cost function
37    with tf.name_scope('cross_entropy'):
38        # this is our cost
39        cross_entropy = tf.reduce_mean(-tf.reduce_sum(y_ * tf.log(y), reduction_indices=[1]))
40
41    # specify optimizer
42    with tf.name_scope('train'):
43        # optimizer is an "operation" which we can execute in a session
44        train_op = tf.train.GradientDescentOptimizer(learning_rate).minimize(cross_entropy)
45
46    with tf.name_scope('Accuracy'):
47        # Accuracy
48        correct_prediction = tf.equal(tf.argmax(y,1), tf.argmax(y_,1))
49        accuracy = tf.reduce_mean(tf.cast(correct_prediction, tf.float32))
50
51    # create a summary for our cost and accuracy
52    tf.scalar_summary("cost", cross_entropy)
53    tf.scalar_summary("accuracy", accuracy)
```

Sample of TensorFlow code

AI Education

Universities have transitioned from being the focal point of AI research to educating a generation of AI engineers. The universities listed below have AI programs.[17] The education

Arizona State University
Auburn University
Ball State University
Brandeis University
Brigham Young University
Brown University
Boston University
Carnegie Mellon University
California Institute of Technology
Colorado State University
Columbia University
Cornell University
Dalhousie University
DePaul University
Drexel University
Duke University
Georgia Institute of Technology
Georgia State University
Harvard University
Indiana University
Iowa State University
Johns Hopkins University
Kansas State University
MIT
Michigan State University
Mississippi State University
Mississippi State University
New Jersey Institute of Technology
New Mexico State University
New York University
North Carolina State University
Northwestern University

The Ohio State University
Oregon Health & Science University
Oregon State University
Pace University
Purdue University
Rensselaer Polytechnic Institute
Rice University
Rutgers University
Stanford University
State University of New York, Buffalo
Syracuse University
Temple University
Texas A&M University
Texas Tech University
Tufts University
Tulane University
University of Alabama in Huntsville
University of Arkansas
University of California, Berkeley
University of California, Davis
University of California, Irvine
University of California, Los Angeles
University of California, San Diego
University of California, Santa Cruz
University of Central Florida
University of Chicago
University of West Florida
University of Georgia
University of Illinois, Chicago
University of Illinois, Urbana Champaign
University of Iowa

---

[17] See the AI International website: http://www.aiinternational.org/universities.html

of AI engineers has gone well beyond Carnegie Mellon, MIT, and Stanford.

University of Kansas
University of Kentucky
University of Louisville
University of Maine
University of Maryland, College Park
University of Maryland, Baltimore
University of Massachusetts
University of Michigan
University of Minnesota
University of New Hampshire
University of New Mexico
University of Oregon
University of Pennsylvania
University of Pittsburgh
University of Rochester
University of South Carolina
University of Southern California

University of Southern California Information Sciences Institute
University of Southern California Institute for Creative Technologies
University of Tennessee, Knoxville
University of Texas, Austin
University of Texas, Dallas
University of Utah
University of Vermont
University of Virginia
University of Washington
University of Wisconsin, Madison
University of Wisconsin, Milwaukee
Washington University in St. Louis
Wayne State University
Worcester Polytechnic Institute
Wright State University
Yale University

There are currently thousands of young software engineers planning a career in artificial intelligence. Forward thinking organizations in almost every line of work are hiring these people to take them into the AI age.

9. A FEW EXAMPLES OF CURRENT AI WORK

The press pays a great deal of attention to the AI efforts of the big technology players: Google, Facebook, Microsoft, Apple, Amazon, and The People's Republic of China. Receiving less notice is the impact of thousands of recent AI capable entrepreneurs applying AI to every corner of the economy. The few examples below give a hint as to what is coming in the next decade or two.

With new technologies, it can be difficult to get an objective assessment of their viability. The stories that appear in news outlets often smell like they were crafted as promotional pieces by the tech companies themselves. With that preamble, I will pass along the best descriptions I can find, some directly from the tech company's website, others from various tech writers.

Law: eBrevia

eBrevia is one of many startups supplying artificial intelligence services to law firms. They focus on "making sense of contract documents." Their web site asserts:

> *eBrevia uses industry-leading artificial intelligence, including machine learning and natural language processing technology, developed in partnership with Columbia University to extract data from contracts, bringing unprecedented accuracy and speed to contract analysis, due diligence, and lease abstraction.*

71

USE ARTIFICIAL INTELLIGENCE TO QUICKLY GAIN INSIGHTS INTO YOUR LEGAL DOCUMENTS

Health: Arterys Medical Imaging

Arterys provides analysis of cardiac images through their cloud services. The following description appeared on the FierceBiotech website.[18]

> *Arterys nabs second FDA OK for deep learning, image analysis software*
>
> *The Arterys Cardio DL software automates time-consuming analyses of cardiac MRI images, generating editable contours showing the inside and outside of the ventricles of the heart. The software processes a scan in 10 seconds, far more quickly than a clinician would. The application uses a deep learning algorithm that was trained using data from several thousand cardiac cases, the company said in a statement. The algorithm produces results comparable to those of an experienced clinical annotator, Arterys said.*

Health: Deep Patient

In 2015, a neuron-based AI system called Deep Patient was trained using 700,000 patient records at Mount Sinai

---

[18] Source: FierceBiotech at http://www.fiercebiotech.com/medical-devices/arterys-nabs-second-fda-ok-for-deep-learning-image-analysis-software

Hospital in New York. The system proved broadly effective at predicting the future health states of 69,214 patients. Deep Patient was developed by a team of doctors and information engineers at the Dudley Lab at the Icahn School of Medicine at Mt. Sinai Hospital. It is an unsupervised deep learning network that predicts future health states of patients from their medical records.

Deep Patient was effective at predicting the onset of schizophrenia in patients. This was particularly interesting since schizophrenia is known to be very difficult for doctors to predict.

Travel: AeroSolve

Hector Lee and Bar Ifrach developed the AeroSolve deep learning AI at Airbnb. (Hector Lee has since moved back to Google.) AeroSolve digests a wide range of relevant information about potential rental properties and offers pricing suggestions to the owners. Owners ultimately set their own price for Airbnb properties. AeroSolve takes into account obvious factors such as the size of the property, location and view. In addition, it factors in assessment of the property's décor by the photographers who provide pictures for Airbnb advertising, rental dates in relation to any special local festivals, and neighborhood type.

The AeroSolve AI has general applicability to pricing problems. The software has been made available at no cost to people like you and me. Their promotional material for the software reads as follows:

Human Friendly, Debuggable Models

Aerosolve was designed to make feature engineering fast and painless. A feature transform language gives the developer full control over the features. General additive models provide lots of capacity while enabling easy interpretation.

Chatbots: Motion AI

Chatbots are AIs that can interact with humans on-line or on the telephone to answer questions or solve problems in a narrow problem area. Motion AI founded by David Nelson in Chicago, focuses on specific areas like restaurants. They have also launched a chatbot store, making software available for other developers. Nelson founded Motion AI in 2015 at age 22. He launched his first venture, Musiic, a streaming music application, at age 15.

Fact Checking: Factmata

Four guys with degrees in machine learning from University College, London have created Factmata, a service that fact checks news articles and political speeches. The website summarizes their mission as follows:

Reducing online misinformation using artificial intelligence.

Factmata is built upon cutting-edge academic research in natural language processing and information retrieval. We are launching a state-of-the-art fact-checking system using machine intelligence, for statistical claims made in digital media content, such as news articles and political speech transcripts.

Our first goal is to make fact-checking more automated, more fun and easier. We want to build a product that engages people in the process of correcting news articles, identifying fallible claims, and supporting more accurate information on the web.

Story Telling: Quill

Quill is an AI system that creates stories from data. Its first incarnation, StatsMonkey, was developed by a team at Northwestern University in 2010. StatsMonkey creates sports stories from data about sporting events. The team went on the create Narrative Science, Inc. The following is a sample story written by StatsMonkey:

Friona fell 10-8 to Boys Ranch in five innings on Monday at Friona despite racking up seven hits and eight runs. Friona was led by a flawless day at the dish by Hunter Sundre, who went 2-2 against Boys Ranch pitching. Sundre singled in the third inning and tripled in the fourth inning ... Friona piled up the steals, swiping eight bags in all ...

Quill is being marketed to organizations to write stories based on corporate operating data. Below is a promotional piece for Quill:

Narrative Science is humanizing data like never before, with technology that interprets your data, then transforms it into Intelligent Narratives at unprecedented speed and scale. Turn your data into an actionable, powerful asset you can use to make better decisions, improve interactions with customers, and empower your employees.

10. QUESTIONS ABOUT THE FUTURE

What Jobs Will AI be Doing?

A study by McKinsey & Company argues that each job involves many types of work, some of which are more susceptible to automation than others. For example, legal work can entail reviewing of massive numbers of documents during the discovery phase of litigation. AI can substantially automate that process. However, courtroom argument in jury trials seem safe from the intrusion of robots.

The chart on the following page gives McKinsey's assessment of the potential for automation in major sectors of work. It defines a range of activity types from *managing* to *predictable physical work*. Activities at the *managing* end of the spectrum are far less susceptible to automation than *predictable physical work*. For each of nineteen broad sectors of work, it graphically shows the fraction of each activity type that makes up that sector. The bars on the right side of the chart indicate the overall potential for automation of each sector. The McKinsey analysis shows that 45% of existing work could be replaced by currently available automation technologies. It does not project the potential for development of more widely applicable artificial intelligence.

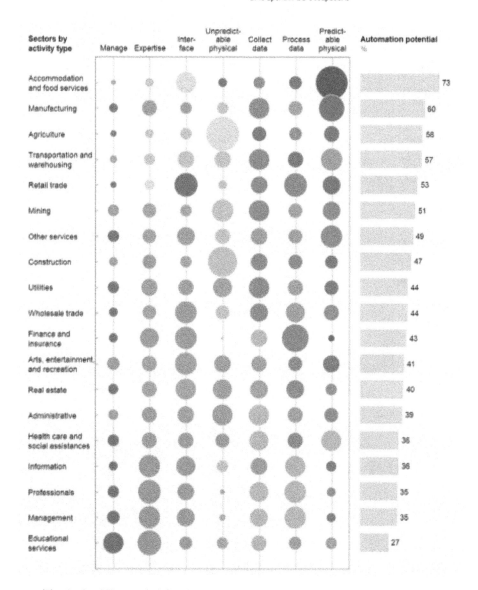

Size of bubble indicates % of time spent in US occupations

Sectors by activity type	Manage	Expertise	Inter-face	Unpredict-able physical	Collect data	Process data	Predict-able physical	Automation potential %
Accommodation and food services								73
Manufacturing								60
Agriculture								58
Transportation and warehousing								57
Retail trade								53
Mining								51
Other services								49
Construction								47
Utilities								44
Wholesale trade								44
Finance and insurance								43
Arts, entertainment, and recreation								41
Real estate								40
Administrative								39
Health care and social assistances								36
Information								36
Professionals								35
Management								35
Educational services								27

Technical Potential for Automation: McKinsey & Company

Eric Weinstein

Eric Weinstein is manager of Thiel capital and a Math PhD from Harvard. He sees AI taking over the vast majority of routine work, the kind of work from which careers are built. He offers that our education system has evolved to prepare people for a career of routine work, where physical and mental expertise is learned at a young age and refined over years of repetitive practice. Weinstein feels that humans are actually far better suited to adapting to unique situations and will be able to compete effectively with computers in performing non-repetitive tasks.

> *I think this means we have an advantage over the computers, specifically in the region of the economy which is based on one-off opportunities. Typically, this is the province of hedge fund managers, creatives, engineers, anyone who's actually trying to do something that they've never done before. What we've never considered is how to move an entire society, dominated by routine, on to a one-off economy in which we compete, where we have a specific advantage over the machines, and our ability to do what has never been done.*

Will AI Widen the Income Gap?

Technology has been making humans more productive for centuries. When productivity increases, either we make more stuff with the same labor, or we make the same amount with less labor. This means loss of jobs. In the first decade of the 19th century, the Luddites rebelled against the automation of the British textile industry. In the long term, new jobs sprung up, but the transition was painful. The core complaint of the Luddites was not so much the increase in automation but what they deemed the unfair profit made by the industrialists.

The chart below shows that the fruits of steady productivity growth in the US economy have not been evenly shared across income levels over the last forty years.

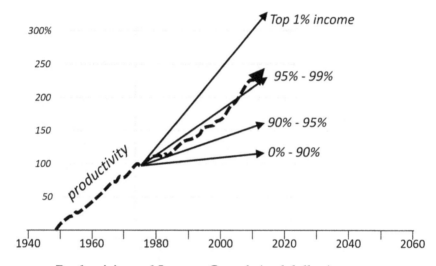

Productivity and Income Growth (real dollars)

Economic Policy Institute 2015

There is every reason to believe that productivity will continue to rise as application of new technologies, particularly AI, becomes more widespread.

Will there always be new jobs to replace those lost to AI?

Elon Musk took the stage at the 2017 summer meeting of the National Governors' Association. He offered predictions on renewable energy, self-driving cars and space travel.

But none were as stark as his views on the future of artificial intelligence.

Robots will be able to do everything, bar nothing.

Musk did not predict a date for when all jobs would be handled by robots, but it is worth considering this eventuality as a thought experiment. If robots were to do all the work, all income will accrue to the owners of the robots. In order to have a functioning economy, either there will have to be huge transfers of wealth from the robot owners to everyone else, or everyone will have to be a robot owner.

Will AI Jobs Takeover Lead to a Downward Spiral in Consumption?

The loss of jobs is not just a problem of an increasing divide between the haves and the have-nots. Economies are driven by consumption. An economy only grows if consumption grows. Consumption requires that money be in the hands of people who will spend it. Income inequality hurts not only the lower income folks, but hurts everyone in an economy that is in decline.

Robocalypse

In June 2017, the rise of robots was officially taken up by a meeting in Sintra, Portugal, of the most powerful central bankers in the world.[19] The bankers are not yet ready to buy into dark visions in which robots render humans superfluous, but at an exclusive gathering at a golf resort near Lisbon, the big minds of monetary policy were seriously discussing the

---

[19] Google "Robocalypse Now" for news about this meeting.

risk that artificial intelligence could eliminate jobs on a scale that would dwarf previous waves of technological change.

Should AI be Regulated?

Elon Musk has a balanced view of the role of regulation. He feels that regulations are often well intentioned but often outlive their usefulness. In his view, regulations are created in response to persistent threats to health and safety. Since the offending industries put up serious resistance, it usually takes years for effective regulations to be enacted. These delays may cost lives, but society tolerates them because the society as a whole is not threatened. Until now.

In the case of AI, Musk argues that regulators must be proactive, since AI has the potential to threaten humanity as a whole, not just individuals. This requires that regulators and their bosses - politicians - understand AI and the threat that it will ultimately pose. Musk provided no guidance on how the regulation of AI would work.

In an op-ed piece in the *New York Times* in September, 2017, Oren Etzioni proposed three rules to govern the development of AI systems. First, AI systems must obey all laws that apply to humans. Second AI systems must disclose that they are not human. Third, AI systems cannot retain or disclose confidential information without the explicit permission of the source of the information. He points out, as an example, the information that a personal assistant (Siri, Alexa) might be able to collect and market for commercial purposes.

Is AI on the Brink of Achieving Human Intelligence?

The Hype Cycle

The technology tracking firm Gartner imagines that new technologies go through a cycle of inflated expectations followed by a trough of disillusionment, then rising to the plateau of productivity.

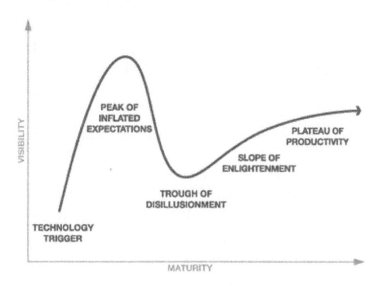

We are left to wonder whether AI has moved through this cycle with the high expectations of the 1970s and 80s, or if we are going through another cycle with the lofty claims for the next twenty years.

Are we really modelling the brain?

In several regards, deep learning networks are inspired by biological neural networks but deviate from them in important ways.

- Human neurons are binary. AI neurons are variable.

- Convolutional layers are invented to retain spatial relations. We are only now learning about grid neurons in the brain and how they might map onto the outside world.
- Neuroscience has a long way to go before we understand the meta structure of the brain.
- Jeff Hawkins is one AI researcher who committed to developing AI techniques that capture brain functions. There are many Hawkins talks on line.
- Computer hardware is moving in the direction of modelling neural networks.

Riza Berkan

Riza Berkan, founder of exClone, Inc. is immersed in application of deep learning to chatbots for businesses. He argues that deep learning as currently practiced by Google is over-hyped as being on the verge of general intelligence. Berkan sees current deep learning technology as being built from digital bricks with only one level of design organization as reflected by the wall segment on the right side of the illustration on the next page. For Berkan, higher levels of AI will require understanding higher levels of cognitive organization as would be reflected in the brick arch spanning the river.

Numenta

In his 2004 book *On Intelligence*, Jeff Hawkins laid out his theory of how human intelligence works. Hawkins assembled his theory out of prevailing ideas in neuroscience. His thinking is based on his understanding of the layered structure of the neocortex. He explains how intelligence could emerge from what seems to be nothing more than a wiring diagram.

After writing the book, Hawkins founded Numenta, a company dedicated to developing artificial intelligence based on our best understanding of how the brain actually works. Of course, that understanding is advancing in parallel with efforts to translate it into computer algorithms. Although the Numenta effort in AI development is small scale compared to that of the major tech companies, Hawkins seems unique in his commitment to capturing the way that the brain actually functions.

Numenta is also committed to spreading the word about what they are doing. Like Google and IBM, Numenta makes its AI software, NewPic, available as open source to anyone. In addition, Numenta engages in an ongoing educational effort to explain the fundamentals of their approach. As of this writing, the twelfth episode of HTM (hierarchical temporal memory) School has been released. HTM is the model of intelligence that Numenta is shaping. It shares many features with other neuron-based AI schemes but is committed to reflecting the latest thinking about brain structure coming out of neuroscience. Matt Taylor of Numenta does a great job of explaining the principles behind HTM and has committed to continuing his series of You Tube performances for at least the next year.[20]

Can Computers be Creative?

Creativity is a trademark of human intelligence. When computers are viewed as automatons slavishly stepping through computer programs, it is hard to see how creativity would emerge. Yet we have several examples of programs that have produced meaningfully creative results.

Brad Dunham's team at IBM came up with a design for the IBM 360 that state of the art engineering practices had not imagined. Design by natural selection is not constrained by logical rules or bound by precedent. Jason Lohn thought the design of his space antenna made no sense at all until it

---

[20] Go to https://numenta.org/htm-school/ for access to all of the HTM School episodes.

was tested and proved to be superior to all previous engineering attempts. Again, natural selection is not bound by assumptions about what a thing should look like.

AlphaGO is the neuron-based AI developed by Google's DeepMind group in London. In 2017, it beat the world Go champion, Ke Jie. When AlphaGo beat Ke in the second of three games, Ke commented:

> *AlphaGo made some moves which were opposite from my vision of how to maximize the possibility of winning. I also thought I was very close to winning the game in the middle but maybe that's not what AlphaGo was thinking.*

Can Neuron-Based AI be Held Accountable?

Logic vs Instincts

Crudely speaking, we could say that rule-based AI is analogous to our conscious, logical mind and neuron-based AI is analogous to our instincts or subconscious mind. When we take actions based on a conscious process, we are able to explain why we decided to do what we did. When our actions are guided subconsciously, which is ninety-nine percent of the time, we rely on our conscious mind to reverse engineer why we did what we did. I have often thought that the main function of the rational mind is to try to figure out (rationalize) why we have done what we have done.

There is concern in the AI community that neuron-based AI systems cannot provide an explanation for their conclusions, recommendations, or the actions that they generate. As discussed earlier, in 2015 a neuron-based AI system called Deep Patient was trained using 700,000 patient records at Mount Sinai Hospital in New York. It proved to be very effective at predicting the onset of schizophrenia in patients. Since schizophrenia is known to be very difficult for doctors to predict, the researchers were very interested in how Deep Patient was able to make these predictions. They still do not know. Joel Dudley, the lead researcher, said: "We can build these models, but we don't know how they work." I think this overstates the case for ignorance. We know how deep learning AI systems work in general, but they do not reveal the clues that lead to their specific conclusions. This is because these clues are buried in the thousands or even millions of synapses that make up the deep learning network.

This is known as the "black box" problem. Experts at DeepMind are exploring methods in cognitive psychology that attempt to infer mechanisms of cognition from behavior.[21]

---

[21] See https://deepmind.com/blog/cognitive-psychology/.

11. Final Thoughts

I find the words of Frank Rosenblatt ringing in my ears, suggesting that Perceptrons are on the brink of achieving true intelligence.

> ... Only one more step of development, a difficult step, is needed ...

And so it is with the artificial intelligence of today. I believe that achieving general artificial intelligence will require several major breakthroughs in our understanding of how our brains achieve their wonders. I also believe that these breakthroughs will come.

It is hard to imagine a world in which the vast majority of what we now consider work will be performed by robots. But imagine you are a farmer in the early nineteenth century. You are among the 74% of the US population engaged in producing food.[22] You are told that in two hundred years only one percent of the population will be involved in food production[23]. You ask what the other 99% will be doing. Well, there will be more than ten times as many people involved in healthcare as in farming. You are in disbelief. The time had not yet come when doctors did more good than harm. Governments at all levels would employ more than

---

[22] Source: Nat'l Bur. of Economic Research   http://www.nber.org/chapters/c1567.pdf
[23] Source: Bureau of Labor Statistics 2014.   https://www.bls.gov/emp/ep_table_201.htm

healthcare. You wonder what all these government people would be doing. One sector of employment after another would baffle you – transportation, financial services, legal services, and hospitality. You wonder how could just a few farmers make enough money to pay for all of these other people.

It has taken 200 years to transition from an agricultural economy to an information economy. The transition to an AI economy will be much faster. Will the jobs that we cannot currently imagine be generated in this compressed period of time?

Finally, will artificial intelligence achieve the flexibility and richness of human intelligence? In my view, this is only a matter of time. And why would AI be limited to matching human intelligence?

GLOSSARY

Artificial Intelligence	The theory and development of computer systems able to perform tasks that normally require human intelligence, such as visual perception, speech recognition, decision-making, and translation between languages.
Backpropagation	The process of strengthening synapses in deep learning networks that lead to correct inferences and weakening synapses that lead to incorrect inferences.
Bit	Element of a binary counting system which uses only 1's and 0's.
Bot	Virtual robot
Byte	A set of bits.
Cerebral Cortex	The largest region of the mammalian brain playing a key role in memory, attention, perception, cognition, awareness, thought, language, and consciousness. (Wikipedia)
Chatbot	A computer program to has dialog with humans by voice or in writing.
Convolutional Neural Network (CNN)	A type of feed-forward artificial neural network in which the connectivity pattern between its neurons is inspired by the organization of the animal visual cortex. Individual cortical neurons respond to stimuli in a restricted region of space known as the *receptive field*. The receptive fields of different neurons partially overlap such that they tile the visual field.
Deep Blue	IBM computer program developed in the 1990s to defeat Gary Kasparov in chess.
DARPA	Defense Advanced Research Projects Agency, an arm of the US Defense Department.
DeepMind	Artificial intelligence company founded in 2010 and acquired by Google in 2014.

Deep Learning	The process of training multi-layered neural networks
Deep Patient	AI system developed to predict health outcomes based on analyzing patient hospital patient data; developed at Mt. Sinai Hospital in New York based on 700,000 patient records.
Frame Theory	A model of human knowledge proposed by Marvin Minsky in 1974. According to this theory, humans organize experience into frames which are then used to make sense of future inputs.
Gigabyte	One billion bytes
Intelligence, Human	The ability to see patterns and predict outcomes based on previous experiences (Jeff Hawkins). This ability is gained from previous experience through learning.
Kilobyte	One thousand bytes
Megabyte	One million Bytes
Neocortex	In the human brain, the neocortex is the largest part of the cerebral cortex which is the outer layer of the cerebrum, with the allocortex making up the rest. (Wikipedia)
Neural Network	A neural network is a massively parallel distributed processor that has a natural propensity for storing experiential knowledge and making it available for use. It resembles the brain in two respects: Knowledge is acquired by the network through a learning process. Interneuron connection strengths known as synaptic weights are used to store the knowledge. (IBM Knowledge Center)
Neuron	An electrically excitable cell that processes and transmits information through electrical and chemical signals. (Wikipedia)
Neuron-based artificial intelligence	Artificial intelligence algorithms based on layers of simulated neurons connected by simulated synapses which learn by varying their strength.

Patterns	Collections of information that must be understood as a whole rather than as a collection of parts.
Pattern recognition	The ability to process complex sensory inputs as a whole.
Perceptron	Early artificial intelligence design. The perceptron algorithm dates back to the late 1950s; its first implementation, in custom hardware, was one of the first artificial neural networks to be produced. (Wikipedia)
RAM	Random Access Memory. Computer memory where programs and data are stored while programs are running.
Rule-based artificial intelligence	Artificial intelligence algorithms that are programmed to capture knowledge and logical operations
Synapse	A structure that permits a neuron (or nerve cell) to pass an electrical or chemical signal to another neuron. (Wikipedia)
Terabyte	One trillion bytes
Training, supervised	The process of exposing a neural network to inputs that are labeled.
Training, Unsupervised	The process of exposing a neural network to unlabeled inputs, leaving it up to the network to group similar inputs into classes.
Unsupervised deep learning	See Training, Unsupervised
Watson	IBM system of computer algorithms designed to answer questions by searching an appropriate knowledge base.